The Illustrated Story of President

BRIGHAM YOUNG

Great Leaders of The Church
of Jesus Christ of Latter-day Saints

The Illustrated Story of President Brigham Young
Great Leaders of The Church of Jesus Christ
of Latter-day Saints

Copyright © 1982 by
Eagle Systems International
P.O. Box 508
Provo, Utah 84603

ISBN: 0-938762-02-8
Library of Congress Catalog Card No.: 82-70264

First Printing April 1982

First Edition

Lithographed in U.S.A.
by
COMMUNITY PRESS, INC.

A Member of
The American Bookseller's Association
New York, New York

The Illustrated Story of President

BRIGHAM YOUNG

Great Leaders of The Church of Jesus Christ of Latter-day Saints

AUTHOR
Della Mae Rasmussen

ILLUSTRATOR
B. Keith Christensen

DIRECTOR AND CORRELATOR
Lael J. Woodbury

ADVISORS AND EDITORS
Paul & Millie Cheesman
Mark Ray Davis
L. Norman Egan
Annette Hullinger
Beatrice W. Friel

PUBLISHER
Steven R. Shallenberger

A
Biography Of
BRIGHAM YOUNG

Brigham Young was the second President and Prophet of The Church of Jesus Christ of Latter-day Saints. He was born June 1, 1801, in Vermont to John and Abigail Howe Young. His family was very poor, and he learned to work hard early in his life. Brought up strictly by his parents, he grew to have a firm faith in Jesus Christ.

When Brigham reached maturity, he was about five feet ten inches tall, with a strong, stocky physique and reddish hair. He worked as a glazier and as a carpenter during his early adulthood.

Brigham was diligent in his study of religion and was very interested when he read about Joseph Smith and his "Golden Bible" in a newspaper article. He obtained a copy of the Book of Mormon, weighed the matter for a year and a half, and then came to a sure knowledge of the truth of the book. A few months after his baptism and confirmation on April 14, 1832, he went to Kirtland, Ohio, to visit the Prophet Joseph Smith. He rejoiced at the privilege of shaking the hand of a prophet of God and received a sure testimony by the Spirit of Prophecy.

Brigham Young served missions for the Church in Canada from 1832-33, in the Eastern States in 1836 and 1843, and in Great Britain from 1839-41. He was ordained an apostle on February 14, 1835, at the age of thirty-three. In this capacity he served for twelve years. He was President of the Council of the Twelve Apostles from April 14, 1840, to December 27, 1847. On December 27, 1847, at the age of forty-six, he was sustained as President of The Church of Jesus Christ of Latter-day Saints. He was President and Prophet for 30 years, the longest administration in Church history.

As persecution of the Saints increased in Nauvoo, Illinois, Brigham Young organized a westward exodus to find a place of safety for his people. He has been called an American Moses by some historians for the way he led his people through the wilderness to their promised land. He is considered the greatest colonizer of the Western United States. Under his direction thousands of pioneers immigrated and settled in the Western deserts and mountain valleys. There, through their faith and diligence, they developed fine farms and beautiful cities. At the same time Brigham Young continually schooled them in the principles of the gospel of Jesus Christ. Today he is recognized all over the world as a dynamic and brilliant leader.

Brigham Young enjoyed social occasions and cultural events. He was an interesting and knowledgeable individual. Brigham Young had plural wives and many children, whom he loved with great devotion.

He chose the site for the Salt Lake Temple soon after the Saints arrived in the Salt Lake Valley on July 24, 1847. He caused temples to be built, organized Church auxiliaries, and founded Brigham Young Academy in Provo, Utah. He strengthened the priesthood quorums and began a more effective organization of the stakes of the Church. Because of his great faith, devotion, and courage, many people called him "The Lion of the Lord."

He died in Salt Lake City, Utah, August 29, 1877, at the age of seventy-six.

John Young looked down at the infant boy lying in the arms of his wife, Abigail. "Well," he said, "we have a fine new son, Abigail. It'll take some hustle to keep food on the table for our nine little ones, but he's welcome!" Abigail answered, "Yes, and I thank God he is well and strong." John asked, "What shall be his name?"

"Let's call him Brigham."

"Brigham . . . Brigham Young . . . a goodly name," said his father.

The date was June 1, 1801. The Young family was living on a farm in Wittingham, Vermont. Only two years later John Young moved his family to Smyrna, Chenango County, New York. The family was poor, and every member had to help. Little Brigham learned quickly. It went something like this:

"Brigham, come help mix the bread."

"Son, after you milk the cows, there is butter to churn."

"Your father needs your help, Brigham, to pick up brush."

"Brigham, we must clear some new acreage."

So the boy picked up brush, chopped down trees, and rolled logs. Sometimes after a day of this work he had bruised shins, feet, and toes. But there is no record that he ever complained.

Brigham had only eleven days of schooling, but he was determined to learn. He taught himself by reading, talking, listening, and working. Brigham admired his father and mother. His father worked very hard to take care of the family. In the evening Abigail Young gathered her family around her to read from the Holy Bible. It was at his mother's side in these twilight hours that Brigham developed a strong religious character. He came to revere his Heavenly Father and Jesus Christ.

When Brigham was fourteen years old, his beloved mother died. It was a time of sadness for the young boy. He said of her, "No better woman ever lived in this world."

After the death of his mother, Brigham made his way alone. Although he was only fourteen, he thought, "I can take care of myself. I know how to work, and I intend to make something of myself." He set about to learn some useful trades. By the time he was twenty-two, he could work as a carpenter, joiner, painter, and glazier. He had become a strong and capable man.

At this time Brigham lived in Port Byron, New York. On October 8, 1824, he married Miriam Works. He had turned twenty-three years of age and had become rather prosperous. One friend said, "Brigham Young is a fine speciman of manhood. He will make his mark wherever he goes."

Just a few years later Brigham moved to Mendon, New York, where several of his brothers and sisters lived. One day he heard some people talking about a "Golden Bible."

"Why," said one man, "there's a man called Joseph Smith who claims he found some gold plates covered with strange writing."

Said another, "I hear Smith has translated the characters into English and published it in a book. He calls it the Book of Mormon."

Brigham was interested in these rumors. A few weeks later someone gave him a copy of the book. He read it at once. Then he read it again. He thought and thought about it. Finally he went to see his brother Phinehas.

"Phinehas," he said, "I have studied this book. I have weighed the matter for a long time. I have looked at it on all sides. I have reasoned on it month after month. I am convinced that there is something in this new religion, 'Mormonism.' "

It was not until the following year that two Mormon missionaries came to Mendon. "We have come to preach the everlasting gospel, as revealed to Joseph Smith the Prophet," they said. Brigham listened. Then he said to them, "I hear and I believe. I have gained a sure knowledge of its truth."

Brigham was baptized on a cold and snowy April day in 1832. From that day on Brigham gave all his strength and ability to building up the kingdom of God.

Brigham was busy and happy, but one thing was missing. He had never met the Prophet Joseph Smith. Finally that great day arrived. Brigham went with his brother Joseph Young and his friend Heber C. Kimball to Kirtland, Ohio. They went to Joseph's father's home and were told, "Joseph is in the woods, chopping wood." They hurried to the woods and found the Prophet and some of his brothers, chopping and hauling wood. Brigham said, "As I shook the hand of the Prophet of God, I received a sure testimony. By the Spirit of Prophecy I knew that he was a true Prophet. My joy was full."

Joseph said, "Welcome, brethren. I am happy to see you. Let us go up to the house, where we may talk together."

Perhaps some of the men who were there when these two men met thought, "There stand two of the greatest men living in the world. They are not rich or famous. Yet they are giants in the eyes of the Lord."

That evening Joseph Smith called a few of the Brethren together. They talked of the kingdom. At the end of the evening, Joseph said, "Brother Brigham, will you offer a prayer?"

As they knelt in prayer together, to the surprise of all, Brigham spoke in tongues. When they arose from their knees, they excitedly asked the Prophet what had happened to Brigham. Joseph said, "Brigham spoke in tongues. It was the pure Adamic language. It is of God." Then he spoke a prophecy, "The time will come when Brother Brigham Young will preside over this Church." Joseph was overjoyed to welcome Brigham into the gospel of Jesus Christ. By the gift of prophecy he knew that a great man and leader had joined the Church.

14

In September, 1833, Brigham moved to Kirtland, Ohio, the headquarters of the Church. Brigham's wife, Miriam, had died, leaving him with two children—Elizabeth, age seven, and Vilate, age two. Brigham married Mary Ann Angell, who made a good home for Brigham and his two little daughters. They were a happy family once more.

In Kirtland the people admired Brigham. They said, "He works hard. He helps the Prophet Joseph in the work of the kingdom." When hard times came, some of the men left Kirtland to look for work in other towns. But Brigham would have none of that. "I came to Kirtland because I was called by the Prophet Joseph. I will not leave here for another place. I put my trust in God that I can earn my living here."

Just at that time a man named Brother Cahoon asked Brigham to build a house for him. Brother Cahoon said, "Money is scarce. I do not know when I can pay you for the work, Brigham." Brigham told Mr. Cahoon, "I will build your house for you. I have faith in God and I have faith in you." Before the house was finished, Brigham was paid in full. Brigham always had great faith in God, in himself, and in other people.

When Brigham had been a member of the Church only three years, the Quorum of Twelve Apostles was organized. He was chosen as an apostle. A group of people stood talking. One said, "I am not surprised. Brigham makes more good sense than most, and he is devoted to God." Another friend added, "That is true. But he is not a long-face. He is jovial and full of fun." A woman said, "I have heard that sometimes the Prophet Joseph calls upon Brigham and his brother Joseph Young to sing duets for him." "Well," laughed another, "it sounds as if Brother Brigham can do just about anything."

One day soon after this Brigham said to his wife, Mary Ann, "My dear, I have been called as a missionary to the Eastern States." Mary Ann knew that he must fulfill this calling. Brigham labored in the Eastern States during the summers of 1835 and 1836. In the winters he came back to Kirtland and worked as a carpenter to support himself and his family.

Heavy trials were soon to come to the Saints. Some people did not like it when the Prophet Joseph said he had seen God. They began to hate the Mormons. Wicked men tried to kill the Prophet Joseph. Both Brigham and the Prophet had to run for their lives. There were troubles in other places, too. Joseph said, "Brigham, we must move the Saints from Missouri. I have received word that mobs come among our people there to hurt and kill them." Brigham worked night and day to help the people escape from the Missouri mobs.

The Prophet looked for another place for the Saints to live. He decided upon Illinois as the new headquarters of the Church. Brigham and the other Brethren hurried to join the Prophet once again. They organized the people and set to work to build a beautiful city, which they named Nauvoo.

Brigham said to Mary Ann, "The mob has taken almost everything we own, but I intend to build a comfortable brick home here in Nauvoo for you and the children. Would you like that?" Mary Ann hardly had time to say yes before Brigham was called with the rest of the Council of the Twelve to serve as a missionary to England. It was the fall of the year 1839 and the weather was growing cold. It was a hard time for the Young family. There was a new baby only ten days old. The whole family had been ill. Brigham had no money, but he said, "I can make me a cap out of this old pair of pants. I do not have an overcoat, so I shall wrap a quilt about my shoulders for warmth."

Brigham was ready to go. He set off on his mission, sick, poor, with hardly a scrap of clothing to his name. But, as always, his faith was strong. He intended to give himself with all his heart to the cause of the Lord. He was determined to go to England to preach the gospel, and that is what he did. No one ever worked harder. He constantly encouraged the other Brethren, and when their mission was finished they had accomplished more than any group of missionaries had ever done before. They baptized between 7-8,000 people. They organized the Saints in many of the towns and cities of England. They arrived at their homes in Nauvoo on July 1, 1841, having been gone for one year and sixteen days. Their families and friends laughed and cried and kissed them. The Prophet Joseph was there to greet them. Brigham was happy to see the growth of Nauvoo the Beautiful. It had become the largest city in Illinois, with 10,000 people.

Brigham said to his wife, "My dear, I am sorry I had to leave you in an unfinished log cabin. It is time for you to have that comfortable home I promised you." He set to work immediately, and when Brigham worked, things happened! Soon a sturdy, brick home was ready. He was also busy plowing his farmlands. And, as always, the Prophet Joseph counted on Brigham to help plan for the Church. Brigham was constantly traveling and preaching the gospel.

On one such trip in June of 1844 he was in the East to ask the Saints for money to help build the Nauvoo Temple. There Brigham received the sad news that the Prophet Joseph had been killed by a wicked mob. Brigham's first concern was for the Church. He remembered the Prophet had said, "I have laid the foundation and you must build thereon, for upon your shoulders the kingdom rests." Brigham slapped his hand down on the table and said, "The keys of the kingdom are here with the Church. We must go on." He gathered the other apostles around him. He knew that the Quorum of the Twelve was the governing body of the Church. "We must hurry back to Nauvoo," he told them. At a meeting of the Saints the day after they arrived home, a vote was taken. The Quorum of the Twelve was sustained as the Presidency of the Church, with Brigham Young as President of the Twelve. As Brigham stood up, the people were astonished. "Look!" they said. "It is as if the Prophet Joseph were standing there."

"His face is the face of the Prophet."

"When Brigham speaks, it is the voice of the Prophet Joseph."

The people knew they had seen a heavenly manifestation. Brigham was happy to have the vote of the Saints. "We will follow the directions of Joseph," he said, "for to him the gospel was revealed in its purity and fullness."

THINK ABOUT IT:

1. Tell about Brigham Young's childhood years. What were some of the things he learned to do?
2. Tell about at least two important things that happened when Brigham Young met Joseph Smith.
3. One of the strongest characteristics of Brigham Young was faith in himself, in God, and in other people. Tell about some experiences that show his great faith.

He called the people together, "We must all sacrifice to complete our beautiful temple. We must have our temple blessings." How the people worked! Early and late. Men, women, and children. In May of 1845 the capstone of the temple was laid. There was great rejoicing and celebrating.

Brigham was quiet, for he knew that an even greater task lay ahead. He knew that he must prepare the people to move from Nauvoo to the West. Mobs and persecutions were increasing. Brigham told the other Brethren, "There will be no peace for us here. Let us organize the Saints into groups of one hundred. We need wagonmasters, carpenters, and blacksmiths to build wagons. We must work night and day, for we must leave for the West as soon as possible."

He talked with his friend Heber C. Kimball. "We will study maps of the West. We will read the reports of travelers and explorers. We must lead this people to a safe, new home."

Brother Heber Kimball said, "Our trip will be a hard one, over plains and mountains and deserts. In some places there will be no water. Indians roam the prairies. There are wild animals and poisonous snakes. We must prepare well for all the dangers."

Brigham was not afraid of these dangers. Over and over again he said to the people, "Have faith and all will be well."

By February 15, 1846, about 3,000 of the Saints were ready to leave. Brigham helped his own family into a wagon. He took whatever possessions he could carry. He gathered up his horses and cattle. He had sold his brick home for six hundred dollars. Then he said good-bye to his farm, his business, the beautiful temple, and the grave of his beloved friend, the Prophet Joseph.

It was a bitterly cold day as the Saints crossed the Mississippi River on the ice to the Iowa side.

Imagine Brigham standing alone in the cold wind, looking westward. Imagine him saying a prayer, "Dear God, help me to lead this people to a safe place in the mountain valleys of the West. They need a place of rest so that they may worship thee in freedom and peace."

But Brigham was not one to be solemn. He knew the people needed encouragement. He had an idea! The Nauvoo Brass Band left Nauvoo on the same day as Brigham and they journeyed together to the "Camp of Israel." When the first camp was established that evening, Brigham called out, "Sound the trumpet to call the camp to a concert." There in the open air and in spite of the bitter cold, the Nauvoo Brass Band started to play its best music. The pioneers began to feel the spirit of the music and soon they were joyously singing and dancing.

Think of traveling with that caravan of 3,000 people as they journeyed across Iowa towards Council Bluffs. They sometimes covered only two to five miles in a day. Sometimes it snowed. Some died and were buried along the trail. They were cold, hungry, and saddened by the loss of loved ones. But always Brigham rode among them, giving encouragement and inspiration. Led by Brigham Young, they actually sang as they trudged along. The days began with song and prayer. The weariness and pain of the day were danced and sung away around the campfire.

Then one day a strange thing happened. The government that had allowed persecution of the Saints sent word that the Mormons must furnish 500 men to serve in the United States Army in the Mexican War. Brigham thought and thought. Finally he said, "We must answer this call. We must send 500 volunteers to serve the country. I promise that I will try to care for the families of these men. I will feed them as long as I have anything to eat myself." So the men of the Mormon Battalion marched off, leaving their wives and children behind. President Young had chosen to support the government that had done little to protect his people.

The largest body of the Saints made a camp at Winter Quarters in Iowa. Brigham decided to lead a small advance party of 143 men, 3 women and 2 children to search out a home in the Great Basin, west of the Rocky Mountains. In Wyoming they met Jim Bridger, a famous Western explorer. He tried to discourage President Young from settling in the Great Basin. He said jokingly, "I will give one thousand dollars for the first bushel of corn grown there!" President Young thought to himself, "This man will be surprised." Aloud he said, "Just wait a year or two and we will show you what can be done." Brigham Young knew that the Lord would help his people. They would make the desert valleys "blossom as the rose."

The little band pushed on, week after weary week, until July 24, 1847. Brigham had fallen ill and was lying down in one of the wagons. As the pioneers came through a mountain canyon, the valley of the Great Salt Lake came into view. The wagons rolled to a stop. Brigham raised himself up and looked out over the valley. It was as if he had already seen it in a vision. He said, "This is the right place. Drive on."

Brigham went to work at once to determine the location for the new city. He decided how the lands were to be divided. Then he knew he must return to Winter Quarters to lead the rest of the Saints to their new home. He left some men in charge in Salt Lake Valley. He took a few men with him and they began the long, dangerous journey back to Winter Quarters. They arrived safely on October 31, 1847, although one night Indians stole twenty-eight of their horses. The Saints were overjoyed and crowded around their leader. Brigham told them, "We have traveled more than 2,000 miles and have found a place where the Saints can live in peace." The people worked hard to prepare during the winter. When spring came, the company started westward. It had 397 wagons, 1,229 people, 74 horses, 19 mules, 1,275 oxen, 699 cows, 82 dogs, 3 goats, 10 geese, 2 beehives, 8 doves, and 1 crow. Just imagine this band of pioneers with their flocks and herds as they started out into the wilderness with Brother Brigham at the head. He probably looked like a modern Moses leading his people into a "promised land."

At the beginning the "promised land" was not very promising. The land was a desert. To make crops grow, water had to be brought by irrigation ditches. The men hunted wild animals to feed their families. Sometimes people dug up sego lily roots to eat. Times were so hard that one group of Saints thought it would be better to move on to California. President Young stood before the people and spoke powerful words: "I know that some of you are murmuring. Some have the gold fever and want to go on to California. Some have not the faith to work and make their families comfortable. I tell you that God has appointed this place for the gathering of the Saints. You will do better right here than you will by going to the gold mines. I promise you that those who leave will wish they had not gone away. Those who stay will prosper and build up the kingdom of God. This is the appointed place!" In this way Brigham inspired most of the people to stay in the Salt Lake Valley.

THINK ABOUT IT:

1. How did Brigham Young help keep up the spirits of the people on their difficult journey across the plains?
2. Why did some people call Brigham Young a modern Moses?
3. How can children today follow the example of President Brigham Young?

39

Early in 1849 the Congress of the United States made the valley and surrounding areas a territorial government to be called by the name of Deseret. Brigham Young was appointed the first governor of the new territory. In the next few years thousands of people came to the valleys of the mountains.

Brigham directed the settlement of many cities and towns. He watched over his people, their houses, their farms, and their flocks. He taught them how to be thrifty and to work hard. He established schools and colleges. He guided the building of the great Salt Lake Temple. He took care of his own large family of wives and children. He preached the gospel with power and authority. It seemed as if all was well for the Saints. Then new trouble came.

Word had reached Washington that the Mormons were rebelling and breaking Federal laws. These charges were false, but a United States Army was sent on its way to the territory to put down the so-called rebellion. Brigham Young stood before the people. He was angry. He said, "We have been driven from place to place; we have been scattered. We have done nothing but try to be obedient and to strive to worship God. Mobs have murdered our people. Now the army has been sent to destroy innocent Saints." Then he thundered out, "But God Almighty being my helper, *they cannot come here.*" He set about making plans to protect his people.

General Wells of the Nauvoo Legion took men into a canyon east of the Salt Lake Valley. He instructed them to stop the march of the government troops. He gave the command, "Stampede their cattle, set fire to their trains, burn the whole country before them and behind them, blockade the road. But do not take their lives." Fortunately, however, as the government troops came toward Deseret, cold weather set in and the troops stopped in Wyoming until spring. In the meantime the President of the United States received word that the reports of the Mormon rebellion were false. The troops were ordered not to harm the Saints. The Saints were at peace once more.

Brigham had reached the age of fifty-eight. He was described as an honest, good-natured, rather thick-set man. He said to his friends, "I am enjoying my life and am in no particular hurry to get to heaven."

Now it had come to a time when the people did not have to spend all of their energy making a living. Brigham announced, "We shall build a theatre!" "What?" "Build a theatre," he repeated. And that is what they did. They constructed a beautiful building called the Salt Lake Theatre. Brigham Young himself went to almost every performance. He encouraged the members of his family to take part in the plays. He said, "People need relaxation and fun. Whatever helps people to be really happy, the Lord approves."

President Young was fun-loving and encouraged other recreation for the people. He said, "There is no harm in a party. Let the people dance and talk and play, but not do any wrong." They had social gatherings, birthday parties, picnics, corn-husking parties, barn-raising parties, adobe-making parties, molasses candy-making parties, and they made a celebration of putting corn and fruit out to dry.

President Young was growing older. At age seventy-six he traveled to dedicate the St. George Temple. He talked to his beloved Saints: "I feel many times that I cannot live an hour longer. But I intend to live just as long as I can. I do not know how soon the messenger will call for me, but I am determined to die at my work."

On August 29, 1877, after an illness of several days, Brigham's family and friends knew that he was near death. They were standing at his bedside when he looked upwards. He cried out, "Joseph, Joseph, Joseph." Those were his last words. Some people believed that the Prophet Joseph had come to take him home to Heavenly Father.

From all over the country came tributes to President Brigham Young. One man wrote, "He was an outstanding citizen of the world."

The Saints gathered to honor their leader. He had loved and cared for his people. They loved him in return. A historian wrote, "He did not set himself up to be great. He set himself up as a servant of God." Indeed, many people called him, "The Lion of the Lord." It is a good name for President Brigham Young.

TESTIMONY

My testimony is the positive. I know that there are such cities as London, Paris, and New York—from my own experience or from that of others; I know that the sun shines, I know that I exist and have a being, and I testify that there is a God, and that Jesus Christ lives, and that he is the Savior of the world. Have you been to heaven and learned to the contrary? I know that Joseph Smith was a Prophet of God, and that he had many revelations. Who can disprove this testimony? Any one may dispute it, but there is no one in the world who can disprove it. I have had many revelations; I have seen and heard for myself, and know these things are true, and nobody on earth can disprove them. The eye, the ear, the hand, all the senses may be deceived, but the Spirit of God cannot be deceived; and when inspired with that Spirit, the whole man is filled with knowledge, he can see with a spiritual eye, and he knows that which is beyond the power of man to controvert. What I know concerning God, concerning the earth, concerning government, I have received from the heavens, not alone through my natural ability, and I give God the glory and the praise. Men talk about what has been accomplished under my direction, and attribute it to my wisdom and ability; but it is all by the power of God, and by intelligence received from him. . . . (JD 16:46)